The Interim Process

The Role of the Church and the Interim Pastor

The Interim Process

■ ■ ■

The Role of the Church and the Interim Pastor

■ ■ ■

**by
Carl Hart**

■ ■ ■

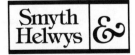
Smyth & Helwys

ISBN 1-880837-01-3

The Interim Process
The Role of the Church and the Interim Pastor
Copyright © 1992 Smyth & Helwys Publishing, Inc.
P.O. Box 72, Greenville SC 29602
All rights reserved

■ ■ ■

■ ■ ■

The paper used in this publication exceeds the minimum requirements of American National Standard for Information Sciences—Permanence of paper for Printed Library Materials.

■ ■ ■

Library of Congress Cataloging-in-Publishing Data

Hart, Carl, 1928–
The interim process :
the role of the church and the interim pastor
by Carl Hart.
x+80 pages. 6x9 in. (15x23 cm.).
ISBN 1-880837-01-3 (alk. paper) : $5.95.
1. Interim clergy. I. Title.
BV4013.H37   1992
254—dc20   92-9064
CIP

■ Contents ■

■ Preface ■

Little has been put in print regarding the interim, that period of time when a church is without a pastor. This book is an attempt to speak to the struggling church and the substitute pastor during the interim time. The author hopes it will provide help for the church and the interim pastor as well as for those who might serve on the pastor search committee.

In no way do I attempt to make this a manual or rule book, but rather an approach to the interim time as I see it. I trust the years I have spent serving in this capacity and my experiences will provide some assistance. I trust, as well, that cases and situations will help others to find identity and thus find direction.

Much credit is due to those churches who have allowed me to serve them during their interim times. Also, credit is due to my wife who I am sure found my involvement in this type of ministry very frustrating at times. Her willingness to listen and help me walk through those touch-and-go times has been extremely helpful. Until recently her involvement was very limited because our two boys needed to have the stability of growing up in our home church. In the past few years she has gone with me exclusively, which I have found to be very helpful. She has been there in her quiet way, not to take a leading role, but to be there to listen, to express care, and to be herself. These comments are to say thanks to my wife, Janie, for her role during the interim times.

I need also to thank and give credit to those who helped me

with the sermons in this book. Laity, ministers, and friends have passed on to me ideas and suggestions for which I am appreciative. I have picked up bits and pieces from more authors than there is space to mention. I give them thanks and trust that I have not abused them too much.

I am grateful for the encouragement and support of Robert J. Rutland without whom I could not have made this book available.

I wish to thank Marcie Brand, my secretary, for typing the manuscript and for the many other things she has done to make this book possible.

■ Foreword ■

Through my years as a layperson, I have noticed many unhappy and happy experiences of churches before and during the interim time. I feel sure that much of the unhappiness could have been avoided if proper guidance had been available and practiced. In this book the author shares his experiences of many years as he has attempted to walk and work with churches during their interim times. He identifies pitfalls and points out dangers. He sees the interim time as a positive opportunity for the church. He keeps the church in the center and the Bible as the authority of the church. In his unique way the author shares experiences that have worked and some that have not worked. All of this is to lay bare before the reader the role of the interim pastor and the task of the church.

The content of this book is far past due. I see it as being very helpful to churches, interim pastors, pastor search committees, pastors, and laypersons as they experience the interim time.

—*Robert J. Rutland*

Chapter 1

The Interim Time Defined

The Interim Time Defined as a Process

Introduction

The interim pastor was greeted on his first Sunday at a church with the words, "I understand you have come to get us back on track."

At another church, the interim pastor was introduced to one of the members who said, "So you are the one who is going to fill in."

Another interim pastor was greeted with the statement, "I sure hope you can straighten us out so we can keep a pastor."

Needless to say, the interim time is in need of clarification and direction. The interim time is not to be treated as a "catch-up" time for the budget, or deserved holidays for the membership, or "Let's do just enough to get us by until we get a pastor." If this is done, the church will cripple its body (the church) and in all likelihood set itself back to a state from which it will take several years to recover. Thus, an understanding of the interim time and the importance of it is imperative if the church is to come out of the process "alive and well."

The interim time is that time when a new pastor is chosen, and that decision may be one that the church membership will have to live with for the next twenty years. Thus the interim period is not a time to be taken lightly. In this fast-food, fast-car, fast-weight-loss age, we do not want to waste any time; we want to call a pastor as soon as possible with as little effort as possible. The interim time is, therefore, sometimes very frustrating, often causing the church to act too hastily without due consideration or research.

The importance of an interim pastor must be stressed at this point. I realize that it takes time even to secure an interim pastor, but an interim pastor is a must. I cannot remember any situation where an interim pastor was not needed.

Some would differ and say, "We have another staff member who can fill that position." This is not advisable because the church may feel it must call the staff member as pastor if this person is doing a fair job. Such a decision does not give the church adequate time to work through the interim process, and time is very important at this point. The church needs time to think, time to release the former pastor, and time to determine the direction of the church for the future. If a staff member attempts to do the job, the people will see the situation as if "everything is fine" and never actually release the former pastor, which will make it very difficult for the staff member. More than likely the congregation will expect the staff person to be a "carbon copy" of the former pastor. In no way is this an attempt to put the staff member down, but rather it is an attempt to look the situation squarely in the eye. The staff member may want to be the pastor of the church, but if this is the case the staff member should refuse the interim task and become available in the same way as the other candidates. The staff person should not in any way confuse or hinder the church with personal desires.

By electing not to secure an interim pastor, the church may think it can rush the process. Some would add that the church could save a great deal of money if different speakers were brought in each Sunday. Many forget that the greater need is to keep the church stabilized. Stability will not be the case when the church is pressured to find someone as soon as possible and when there is a different face in the pulpit every Sunday with a sermon that may not relate at all to the church's needs.

Some churches do not have staff members other than the pastor. Where does a person who needs counseling or other pastoral care go then if there is no interim pastor? Who encourages the church and rallies it behind the pastor search committee? Who can feel the hurt of the congregation who has lost its pastor, and who can walk with the members in their grief? Who can do personal witnessing and baptize converts and perform the various other duties needed week after week? The interim pastor certainly cannot fill the shoes of the pastor; yet such a person can lighten the load, bridge the gap of feelings, love the people, and provide ministry until a pastor is found. Regardless of how capable the different Sunday-after-Sunday speakers may be, the church suffers without an interim pastor.

The Interim Process

The interim time can be looked upon as a process. It is a process that unfolds without being structured or programmed. At the same time, it cannot be coerced or scheduled, but rather it finds its own way if certain conditions exist.

The story has been told of the person who asked a member how far along the church was toward calling a pastor. The church member said, "Well, we are making progress. The church had its mind set on Billy Graham, but we finally realized that was impossible. Then we tried to get a preacher with a doctor's degree in theology, and we found out we couldn't afford one. Then we wanted to find one who had studied Greek; after hearing two or three of those, we realized Greek didn't help us too much. The committee is now looking for an educated, down-to-earth, caring pastor that we can afford. So, we are making progress."

The interim process then could be said to be a progressive approach that will assist the church in its search and selection of a pastor. This process has three clearly defined stages.

First, there must be a time for facing reality and releasing of the former pastor. The pastor has gone. Accepting the fact that the pastor has gone is very difficult for some. Whether the leaving was pleasant or unpleasant, whether the pastor served the church a long time or a short while, the church must deal with the fact that the pastor has gone. It is difficult for the entire church to deal with the matter because there are so many different experiences and memories of the former pastor. Some will need time to grieve. Some will need a time to think things through. Regardless, all will need time and help to release the former pastor and let that particular person go. They need time to give the former pastor credit for all the accomplishments and good that was done and time to forgive the former pastor for all the mistakes or blunders that were made. This will take time. The former pastor baptized children, married couples, and buried parents, and such a person is not easily released.

I began as interim pastor at one church where the pastor had left after serving there for thirteen years. Four weeks after I went there, the committee brought before the church a candidate for pastor. After hearing him preach in the morning worship hour, the congregation asked him to step out and voted him in as the new pastor. Needless to say, the church acted too soon. The membership had not released the former pastor. There were too many memories. Thirteen years is a lot of time to block out in four weeks. The membership had not been given time to grieve, and think, and process the going of the former pastor. Six months later, I was called again by this church because the pastor had resigned. The church had not taken time to release the former pastor and get ready for a new one. In just four weeks there was a new face in the pulpit. The church members did not accept him after they had called him.

One of the purposes of an interim pastor is to help the people get accustomed to a new face preaching to them, and observing the Lord's Supper with them, and walking with them in their daily problems. This takes time.

Some former pastors make it very difficult for the church to release them. I was interim pastor of a church where the former pastor mapped out what he thought the church should do when he left. It appears to me that it would have been very difficult for a church even to think otherwise as far as the future was concerned. Because the former pastor had called upon the members to commit themselves to the goals he had presented, they were locked in. They would forsake both God and their former pastor if they did otherwise. All to say, sometimes the church finds it very difficult to release the former pastor because of an ego-centered departure.

The first step then in the interim process is to release the former pastor. This is not to say that the pastor should be forgotten, but rather "let go." If the pastor is not "let go," it will hinder the work of the pastor search committee because the church will be tempted to compare a candidate for pastor with the former pastor; and it could likely bring confusion and disunity to the church. Time should be given to allow this first step to take place.

How much time? No one can say. It appears that the longer a pastor has served a church, the longer it will take to "let go." How long may also depend on how the pastor left. For example, if the beloved pastor died while preaching, as one I knew did, it seems that it would be very difficult for the membership to "let go" suddenly. No one can set a time because each situation is different. A church can know, however, when it is making progress and "letting go" because the membership will begin to talk about things that relate to the second stage of the interim process.

The second stage of the interim process can be identified as a time for evaluation or seeking direction. There is no better time than the interim time for a church to ask itself, "Where are we headed?" "What have we done wrong?" "What do we want to do in the future?" The answers to such questions can help the pastor search committee to seek a leader who can lead the church to accomplish its goals. Also, the answers to such questions can unify the church and create interest, as well as encourage the members to get ready to support their new pastor.

The church needs time to look at itself and evaluate the state of the church. The pastor search committee can be helpful at this point. The committee can provide a survey and meet with the church council, the deacons, and others to encourage the church to begin to study and plan for the future. This stage is very important because the present staff members can get the feel of the direction of the church which, in turn, will give them security. On the other hand, this will at least help them seek out the direction for their future. In many cases, the present staff can encourage this second stage in the interim process by providing research, meeting with the pastor search committee, and offering other assistance that gives the church a clearer picture of its community and its mission.

The skills of the interim pastor are of great importance at this time. The interim pastor's ability to help the church face up to its potential during this stage could be essential for the church.

I recall one church that for many years had bivocational pastors who lived seventy miles away. They had served the church well, but the community had grown through the years, and changes had brought to the surface new challenges for the church. The skilled interim pastor tactfully led the church to take a look at this. The membership conducted a survey in the community. After prayerful concern and consideration, the church decided to seek a pastor who could serve full time and live in a home in the community. The pastor search committee then had to change its direction because it was given new instructions by the church. This move not only challenged the church, but rather it unified the church and gave the search committee the support and direction that it was lacking.

The above case reminds me of many churches who have locked themselves into situations or traditions that have hindered their outreach. Some pastors, as sincere and committed as they might have been, have locked churches into patterns or visions of the church's role. No better time exists for the church to look at itself than during the interim time. This period can be a time of change and evaluation. But the other side of that coin is for the church to seek the "good old days" or, to put it another way, to go back where there was security or where they did not have to put forth much effort. This accounts for the fact that many churches do not grow in size or challenge. They change pastors over and over and each time go back to the comfort zone. A skilled interim pastor is invaluable at this point to lead the church to constructive observation. The interim pastor will find that it is at this stage that sermons dealing with unity, missions, and stewardship can steer the church to growth.

The third stage in the interim process can be labeled "getting ready for the new pastor." This is a very important part of the process. Maybe it can be illustrated along the lines of a wedding. Once the announcement is made that a couple is getting married, preparation begins and continues right up to the time of the wedding. In a sense, a wedding takes place when a church calls a pastor. The pastor is united to the church to serve for an indefinite period of time. Preparation is very important if the "marriage" of a church and new pastor is to be successful and compatible.

The church should be excited about the new pastor's coming. Part of the joy of a wedding is the excitement of the forthcoming event. The church needs time to get excited. The people need to feel the assurance that they have made the right selection, that the person chosen is God's minister for them, and that the new pastor will bring the leadership they need. They should not see the new pastor as a "miracle person," but as one who is the "groom that the bride has chosen"!

The church will find it helpful to prepare for the new pastor. It needs to make certain that it has taken care of the past. The church should ask, "Are we carrying over anything that we should have handled?" "Is the pastor inheriting any old problems that we have not settled?" "Are there already `two strikes' against the new pastor from the start?" No pastor should be asked to inherit problems that only the church can resolve. A church has not been fair if it has not dealt with everything that might hinder the ministry of the new pastor or the future mission of the church. There is no better time than the interim time to get ready for a new pastor and the future.

The church also prepares for the new pastor's coming by releasing the interim pastor. In the absence of a pastor, it is very easy for a church to become attached to the interim pastor. The interim pastor's messages may be challenging and timely, and this person's caring approach may encourage the membership to become very fond of its interim pastor. Nevertheless, the church must release the interim pastor. This pastor "must decrease and the excitement of the new pastor increase." The skill of the interim pastor to guide the congregation to do this is very important.

I know of one interim pastor who did not want to "let go" and allow the congregation to release him. I recall a church that kept the interim pastor on the staff and made him the associate pastor because the membership would not release him. I might add that he allowed this to happen. No one wanted to hurt anyone.

The point here is not that anyone might hurt someone, but the point is common sense. The new pastor does not need matters of old loyalties regardless of how kind and agreeable the former interim pastor might have been. The new pastor will be in the spotlight enough as it is; the pastor does not need to be compared to the former interim pastor. Releasing the interim pastor is difficult at times, but must this be done if the church makes adequate preparation for the coming of a new pastor.

This process may sound too simple for some. Others may say, "We don't have time for all this; let's get on with it." But I cannot emphasize the fact enough: unless healing takes place, be it grief, joy, or whatever, and if evaluation of the state of the church does not take place, and if preparation for the coming of the pastor does not take place, the church sets itself up in most cases for disappointment in the future.

It must be said again that the interim process does not

unfold like a hideaway bed. Rather, it surfaces here and there, sometimes overlapping, in some cases taking more or less time than others. The process will unfold only when it is allowed to do so freely. Thus the church must guard itself and avoid favoritism, politics, and self-interest. Or to state it another way, the church must not allow a single individual or group to lay its claim on the process.

I have served as interim pastor where I succeeded another interim pastor, and I learned after getting there that the church had just appointed its second pastor search committee. Now this says that the process had not started or that it was hung up on step one or two. Or further still, the church might not have had leadership to guide it through the interim process. More than likely it was because an individual or group was attempting to lay claim on the process.

The Interim Process in Motion

This process is set into motion when the membership becomes aware of the importance and responsibilities of the church during the interim time. The church has selected a pastor search committee, but it is important for the members to realize that they, too, are just as responsible as the committee. The committee acts only on behalf of the membership. It is important that members leave the committee alone and allow it to function freely. Their task is to support that committee with constant prayers, patience, and sincere input. Such support from the membership will encourage the pastor search committee as well as keep it moving in the right direction.

The church membership should also realize that during the

interim time it has an added responsibility, and that is to fill in the gap left by the pastor. The pastor was the leader and promoter of the program of the church as well as the shepherd of the flock. The membership must not allow things to coast or just get by. Nothing should be put on hold, postponed, or canceled. A layman once said, "Let's plan and work as if we were never going to get a pastor, but be ready if he comes tomorrow." As was said already, the church could easily set itself back during the interim time, which may well take several years to regain, if it does not realize the importance of this time.

A layman once said to an interim pastor, "I see this as a 'cooling off' period." Maybe he was attempting to say, "I see this as a time when certain things must happen." The church has a responsibility to see this as a time of soul-searching, genuine forgiveness, and recommitment. The church cannot expect God's leadership when it reaches the day to call a pastor if its members are not healed members. Jesus reminded us of this in Matthew 5:24 when he said, "When you come to the altar and remember that your brother has ought against you, go first and be reconciled with your brother and then come and offer your gift."

The interim time is important in that it is a time when the church is called to regroup. As stated earlier, this is a time when the church should look at the direction it is going, asking itself some very important questions such as, "What did we do wrong in the past?" "Where are we headed?" "What are our goals?" "Are we providing an adequate ministry in this community?" "Are we fragmented?" "Are we in a rut?" The interim time is the ideal time for a church to come to grips with itself, to reevaluate itself. This will regroup and unite the membership. It will equip the pastor search committee. It will place responsibility on the church. It will bring challenge to the future. The interim time sets into motion then a call to regroup.

The interim time is a period when spiritual growth can take place. As one church member stated it, "I feel like our church has grown more during the interim time than it has in a long time because it has called our membership to accountability and responsibility." Another said, "Our church is stronger now than it has ever been." The simple fact is that if a church will accept the interim time as a time of healing and a time of regrouping, spiritual growth will take place. The interim process will begin to unfold, thus preparing the church to find the pastor who will "dream dreams and see visions" with the church, as well as a pastor the church can look in the eye and say, "We are ready to follow our shepherd to greener pasture." The interim process takes birth when the congregation gets a feel of its role and responsibility during the interim time.

The Church Accepting the Interim Process

Many things will influence the church as it opens its eyes to the interim process. Tradition, or the "way we have always done it," or dissatisfaction with the way it was done last time, or personal ideas, and many other influences will "rise up and call themselves great" during the interim time. Some of these will hinder and some will help the church move into the interim process.

Certainly the interim pastor can assist at the very outset by preaching to the human needs of the people. The interim pastor will want to deal with subjects like love, joy, forgiveness, and hope. A sermon that I have used to assist at this point is entitled, "Where Do We Go from Here?" Regardless of the situation, the sermon should relate to where the church is and its options for handling the situation. I have found that the church moves into the interim process quickly when positive and affirming sermons are delivered. Negative sermons condemning the church membership will put the interim process on hold in most cases. In a very tactful way, the interim pastor can walk with the congregation through its grief and frustrations with the preaching of sermons that heal. Such help can move the church into the interim process.

Leaders and programs can also assist the church to move into the interim process. I recall the chairman of the deacon body of a church where I once served. He asked me for a few minutes before the worship service to speak to the membership. His words were warm and encouraging. He simply and pointedly gave assurance that the ministry of the church was being covered and that the business of the church was in excellent hands. He closed his remarks with a strong support for the pastor search committee and a commitment of himself during the interim time. You could almost feel the interim process beginning that morning.

I recall one church where I had served as interim pastor for about three months. It seemed as if the church was in a coma until the time came for the emphasis and promotion of the special foreign mission offering. The former pastor had placed much emphasis on this special ministry so the president of the Woman's Missionary Union and myself put together a program of emphasis that was very effective. It accomplished its purpose and the church went over its mission offering goal. At the same time this program helped the church to realize its worth and importance. It created an openness that was essential if the interim process was to begin.

There are times when a revival emphasis can cause the interim process to take root. I recall a deacon saying, "Our church has not had a revival in two years; maybe we need to have one." Now I am not one for revivals during the interim time. I think they should be postponed or canceled. My thinking is that the interim period is a very tense time for the church and should be devoted to prayer and work that will lead to the calling of the pastor. But in this case I felt maybe a revival would help. I agreed and sought a speaker that I thought could help us. His messages were strong, very biblical, and practical. It worked! The fourth night the church responded! Genuine revival broke out, and that church moved into the interim process. From that time on the finding and calling of the right pastor was accomplished with ease.

I see the church council, the deacon body, and the staff starting and/or stimulating the interim process. I usually meet with the deacon body, church council, and the staff as soon as possible after I am selected as the church's interim pastor. I explain to them the importance of the interim time and the interim process. I ask that we allow it to happen, not try to force it upon the church. I ask them to be united and committed in prayer that we all will do our part during this time. I then say little or nothing more about the steps of the interim process. With the church leadership knowledgeable of the goals of an interim pastor, it will indirectly respond and the process, most of the time, will unfold in its own time frame.

Some Models That Characterize the Interim Time

Being able to see the situation at hand a little clearer is always helpful. Most interim pastors begin their tasks blinded. A doctor would first enter the patient into the hospital and have a series of tests run before attempting to offer help. The interim pastor seeking to find out the state of the church, however, would get many different interpretations and an overemphasis on certain conditions. The interim pastor must come in blinded and slowly listen, observe, and without partiality, love the membership. While feeling the way, the interim pastor will notice patterns of response which will enable the assistance of the unfolding of the interim process.

The following are only a few of the many different models that the interim pastor may face. Being able to identify these, and thus being prepared for some of the responses, can be helpful. Like the doctor, the interim pastor can only prescribe the cure when the illness is known.

Sudden Death

On his first Sunday at the church after the pastor had suddenly had a fatal heart attack, the interim pastor said, "I don't believe they heard a thing I said; they just sat there and cried all through the sermon." He added, "I soon realized my first task was to deal with their grief and guilt - grief because they felt they had lost the best pastor they had ever had and guilt because they felt they had pushed him too hard and expected too much from him." Had this interim pastor not picked up on this and dealt with it at the outset, the interim process would have been placed on hold. But being able to see this, the interim pastor walked with them through their grief and guilt, leading them to forgive themselves and to be on their way again as a church.

Burnout

A pastor called one Monday morning and told me he was resigning and had recommended me as the interim pastor. My quick comeback question was, "Why did you resign?" He said, "I have just had enough. The church expects me to do everything. I have not had a vacation since I came here five years ago. I am doing all I can for the church, and the members expect more."

The reception I received on the first few Sundays at that church could be characterized as "dead silence." No one said a thing regarding the church or the former pastor or the future. Finally, it began to come through that they were in shock. "Why would a pastor leave with nowhere to go when things were going well here?" one member asked. To get the interim process started, I felt that I must first help the membership to see that the pastor cannot "be all things to all people." I slowly tried to educate the membership on the role of the pastor.

Staff Conflict

The interim pastor does not usually ask, "Well, why did your pastor leave?" The interim pastor just walks in, saying silently, "What will I find here? Help me, Lord, to be able to help whatever it is that I find."

On one occasion the interim pastor was told on his first Sunday there that the church had fired its three staff members (pastor, minister of education, and music/youth minister). The interim pastor quickly noticed that three groups identified themselves in the church. They were made up of the followers of each of the fired staff members. In fact, each group felt its staff member had been mistreated and should be reinstated. The interim pastor walked that narrow line between the three groups, realizing that he could not identify with either, but somehow had to bring about unity if the interim process was to unfold. Noticing that the adult members were so focused on their feelings (and they were important) that they had failed to see what was occurring with the children and youth who were standing by wondering what was going to happen next, the interim pastor began to focus his attention and messages on the role of the church, its mission, its part in the redemptive process, its helper, the Holy Spirit, and its Head, Jesus Christ. Needless to say, this was not an easy situation. There are times when the interim pastor, too, must "wait on the Lord." In this case, the interim pastor faithfully performed his tasks as best he knew how for eleven months.

Then one night it happened. The attendance was extra good for the evening services, which was usual for this church. The sermon was not much different from others he had preached. But when the invitation was given to rededicate life and service to the church, it was as if someone said, "Will you all come to the altar?" Every member of the church came to the altar. Some could not get close because the altar area was full, and they had to stand in the aisles. The interim process reached a high peak that night. From that time on the process unfolded, and the church soon called a pastor.

Control

It is evident that some churches never keep a pastor very long. They find it necessary every few years to go back to battle to determine who is in control. The pastor is caught in the middle. The pastor may see the battle surfacing and not want to be in such an uncomfortable position, so decides to leave. The battle may continue until the very day the new pastor is called, unless the cycle can be broken. The interesting thing is that the church will usually select a pastor upon whom they will be allowed occasionally to practice their control skills.

There have been churches that called the pastor for only a year. Thus, each year the pastor was called for another year, and this would go on year after year. It was not so much that they wondered if the pastor was going to turn out all right, but rather they wanted to do an annual check to see who had control. The interim process in a situation like this many times does not take place at all. Even the pastor search committee finds itself pulled by the parties seeking to control it. It should be remembered that the interim pastor can say things that a pastor cannot say. It may be that the interim pastor can face the situation and help enough of the membership to become dissatisfied with such games and decide to stop them.

One interim pastor who found himself in a situation like this tactfully preached and taught everything he could find on the authority of the church.

Church and Pastor Abuse

There are times when the church feels that it owns the pastor, and, likewise, the pastor sometimes claims ownership of the church. As one church member told the interim pastor, "He left us high and dry; he took the computer, sound equipment, and the office furniture that was purchased with church funds." A pastor who had resigned his church said, "They starved me to death." Another said, "They put me out and I had nowhere to go." An interim pastor can experience a lot of anger in a situation where abuse has occurred. If such abuse is not dealt with, it could carry over to the next pastor.

On his first Sunday at the new church, one pastor overheard someone say, "I hope this one will leave the church's typewriter when he goes." The interim pastor must pick up on anger caused by abuse of one or the other and help the church to get it behind and out of the way if the interim process is to proceed.

Embarrassment

The interim pastor will find as a part of the pastoral duties the task of going where there has been embarrassment. Some embarrassment comes in surprise packages while some lingers on before becoming public. One interim pastor had to follow an embarrassing divorce of the former pastor who left the church frustrated, broken, divided, and deeply disappointed in the ministry. After three months into the interim, when progress was beginning to be made, the church got the news that the former pastor had married a member of the church. This came as such a shock to the church that the interim pastor had to start over again to help the members face up to the human dimension that is in us all. There are times when only the Sermon on the Mount can clean out our hurt, frustration, and abusive words and thoughts. Some situations take much longer than others to overcome the embarrassment involved, but the patient interim pastor is a minister indeed if he can bring the church around to the point of forgiveness and hope which will allow the interim process to unfold.

Division

The interim pastor noticed that the congregation was smaller than he thought it would be on his first Sunday there. After the service he found out why - the former pastor had taken about half the members with him to start another church. The church suffered even greater hurt when it realized that this happening also split families. In some cases, a husband and wife stayed while the son and daughter-in-law went with the other group. Next-door neighbors were divided with some going and others staying.

The interim pastor will find that there is no formula for a situation like this most of the time. But, as in other situations, the interim pastor does far more listening than talking and giving advice. One interim pastor said that he did not mention the church's situation. He just listened and tried to be a friend.

He said it seemed that after so long the members got tired of talking about their dilemma and hearing others talk about it. So they quit and basically said, "Where do we do from here?" With the friendly relations that the interim pastor had already established, the interim process was ready to move on.

These models are only a few, and those mentioned above take on all types of variations. If, however, they can help us to be more observant and aware of the situations that characterize the interim time, they will have served their purpose.

Expected Results of the Interim Time

The intended results of the interim time and process are to create an atmosphere that will allow God's will to function in the life of the church. If the church can avoid getting caught up in its own destructiveness and self-centeredness and seek ways whereby it can walk through the interim time together as a church family, the intended results will be realized. If the church can identify its hurts and allow the healing of prayer, the preaching of the Word, and fellowship of members, the intended results will have taken place. If the church comes together in unity to find its mission and fulfill its goals, the intended results are already being accomplished.

If the church is prepared to be open and understanding, and if the church can say "God's will is more important for the church than anything else," then the process of the interim time has accomplished its dream. If the church feels good about itself, if it feels healthy again, if it feels that it is ready to reach out and witness and love people back into the fellowship of the church, then the intended results of the interim time and interim process will have been accomplished.

Chapter 2

The Interim Pastor Realizing the Unique Task

The Task of Filling the Gap

Defining the Task

The interim pastor enters this task as a sensitive and caring person. This is one of the first things the membership will notice, and soon they will turn to the interim pastor to talk out postponed hurts and frustrations. Many times people do not select the pastor's office to talk, but will approach the interim pastor in the hallway after the worship service or in a group. The skill of the interim pastor to handle such situations (or sometimes they could be called confrontations) is very important. To walk that fine line between several factions, to encourage, to stabilize, to build morale is the task of the sensitive and caring interim pastor.

Establishing the Role of the Interim Pastor

It is at this point that the interim pastor can help the church begin the interim process or lose it. One's skill to stabilize the church, to calm its pounding pulse and move on with healing is essential. The members will "lick their wounds" until they are led to seek healing. This is the task of the interim pastor. Maybe a challenge would be to deliver a message on the subject, "Enjoying Our Illness."

The underlying task of the interim pastor is to bring stability to the church. This is why it is so necessary that a church carefully select an interim pastor rather than try to just "fill the pulpit." A parade of former pastors, lay ministers, and seminary students to "fill the pulpit" will not bring stability to a church. This approach only provides free advice, pressure on the pastor search committee, and sermons that go nowhere. The consistent appearance of the same person in the pulpit, a sensitive caring person walking among the people, and sermons that relate to needs of the people will bring stability. This is the task of the interim pastor.

Leading in Worship

Worship calls us to think, seek out, and change. Worship must be entered into, experienced, and shared. Worship unites the membership and strengthens the church. Worship does not just happen; it must be worked at diligently. It takes time, planning, and prayer. The task of the interim pastor is to lead the church in successful worship. As indicated in Romans 12, worship is the dedicating of oneself to God. Above all, the interim pastor must try to see that this is accomplished.

Working with the Staff

Also, the task of the interim pastor is to work closely with other members of the church staff. They will feel lonely, overworked, and frustrated. Their questions will be: "What kind of pastor will the church call?" "Will the new pastor want me to continue on the staff?" "What do I do until the new pastor comes?"

The interim pastor seeks ways to work with the staff by helping the staff to feel comfortable and a part of the church program. The interim pastor plans with the staff members and gives them time to share. This involves keeping them informed regarding the interim process. The interim pastor coordinates the pastoral duties involving the staff. The interim pastor will find the church staff a very helpful resource that will assist in fulfilling the interim pastor's own task.

Reaching Out to the People

The interim pastor is not a "handyman." Yet at times this may seem to define best the interim pastor's tasks. On the other hand, the interim pastor must not forget the many aspects of the task of being an encourager and stabilizer. Keeping the church informed, promoting the church program, remembering special days on the church calendar, supporting the youth and children programs, and encouraging the senior adults are all part of the task of encouraging. The interim pastor also encourages the church to pray for the pastor search committee. Encouragement and stabilization involve attending the church council meetings and deacons' meetings, visiting the hospital, or calling by phone when the time is limited. The interim pastor also drops in on other meetings of the church to express interest and concern. One may send out a letter to the church members to encourage them during the interim time. The interim pastor must pray for the church and for its future. Taking the work in all of its dimensions seriously is the interim pastor's task.

The Task of Preaching

The interim pastor is a specialist with a predetermined task, which is to guide the church to use the interim time as a vehicle to accomplish specific goals. The interim pastor fulfills this task primarily by preaching sermons that are helpful. Precious time is wasted if the sermons do not speak to human needs.

Preaching That Is Effective

During the interim time many church members are ready for a change. They want changes to take place in the church, but they also seem to be ready for changes to take place in themselves. They are open, they are willing, and they need help to make the proper responses. On the other hand, there are those who will expect "strong" preaching (most of the time their meaning of this is negative preaching) so that the members might be driven to "get right with God." Others will hope for as little preaching as possible so that they will not feel the need to respond or change in any way. Preaching then by the interim pastor obviously becomes very important.

The interim pastor may be tempted to "warm over" old sermons. This is all right if the sermons speak to the needs of the people and do not become "hand-me-downs,"or "shots-in-the-dark." Maybe I can say it this way - the interim pastor should never be a "peddler of preaching."

I recall a man from my childhood days who lived down the road from us and was a "pill roller." Now a pill roller was a person who claimed to have knowledge enough of the medical field to create tonics and pills from herbs that would improve health and cure all ills. Each Saturday morning this man would take his little satchel to town and peddle his wares on the street corner. The interim pastor must not peddle bits of wisdom that neither cure nor improve, but should use the authority of the calling of God to deliver creative and soul-searching sermons.

Preaching That Is Planned

The interim pastor will find that planning ahead is a helpful practice. Observing the church calendar and taking advantage of special days such as holidays and days of special emphases can help accomplish this purpose. The interim pastor should plan the preaching with the staff and church council so as not to miss an opportunity to support the church's ministry and assist with the interim process at the same time.

I have found it helpful for me to have sermons prepared to preach that will relate to each of the steps of the interim process. I have no special order. I just weave them in as I feel it is appropriate. Doing this, I have found, keeps the process moving in the right direction without pushing. As I have stated, the process must unfold according to its own timetable and cannot be coerced by "strong preaching."

I have never been a captive of my own plans. I try to stay open to what I feel and interpret. The sermon topics listed below, however, are some I have used during the three stages of the interim process.

Stage 1. The Beginning of the Healing Time

"Where Do We Go from Here?"
"Drops of Love"
"Learning to Love Like Jesus"
"A Fresh Look at Forgiveness"
"Joy Is Our Strength"
"When I Grow Up"
"What Is Your Concept of God?"

Stage 2. Evaluating the State of the Church and Determining the Future Direction

"A Heart for Mission"
"How to Be Happy"
"Sin Chains Us"
"God Had Plans for a Boy"
"The Struggling Church in Today's World"
"Has the Church Bought a Horse?"

Stage 3: Getting Ready for the Pastor

"Are We Ready for a Pastor?"
"The Minister and His Message"

"Knowing How to Find God's Will"
"How to Work with Your Pastor"
"How to Welcome Your Pastor"

(Manuscripts of several of these sermons can be found in chapter 3 of this book.)

Planned preaching by the interim pastor will be realized by the membership and this, too, will contribute to the flow of the interim process.

The Task of Stepping Aside

Planning for the End

As the interim process comes to a close, the interim pastor must fade into the background. This must be planned and worked at long before the day that the interim pastor is to leave. It should be stressed that the task of the interim pastor is coming to a close for this is a part of the interim process itself. The interim pastor encourages the membership as it plans and looks forward to the new pastor. Sermons on "How to Work with Your Pastor" and "How to Welcome Your Pastor" give opportunity to do this.

I have participated in services where the new pastor and the interim pastor conducted a service together with the interim pastor greeting the new pastor on the first Sunday by passing on the task of the pastor. At that time the pastor expresses appreciation to the interim pastor for the task done and in behalf of the church releases the interim pastor. Some call this an installation service. This type of service would certainly allow the church to express gratitude to the interim pastor and at the same time experience the official release of the interim pastor, both of which are very important to the membership.

It should be stressed that the interim pastor should cut all ties with the church. The interim pastor does not need to come back to the church unless invited by the pastor. Nor does the interim pastor need to call or write members, asking them, "How is the new pastor doing?"

The Rewards of the Interim Pastor

The interim pastor's reward will not be to keep ties with the church or to count how many church members are considered as friends. But rather reward is found in the fact the church was unified and the mission goals of the church were encouraged. The interim pastor's reward continues through remembering the prayers that were answered and how the trust in fellow members was revived. The interim pastor's reward is to sense the joy that the church experienced as it looked forward with excitement to its new pastor. Thus the interim pastor allows the conclusion of the interim time to be the beginning of a new day for the church, healthy and alive!

■ **Chapter 3** ■

Sermons during the Interim Time

Introduction to Sermons

Already I have attempted to stress the importance of preaching to human needs. Some would say this is pastoral care preaching. Regardless of what it is called, the purpose of the preaching during the interim time is to create an atmosphere and offer direction so that the interim process can work. The interim pastor can approach subjects differently than the pastor. At the same time, the interim pastor is limited by time and must not waste a single opportunity to bring words of healing and direction. With this in mind, the following sermons are some that I have found helpful as I have attempted to work with churches and walk with them during the interim process. These sermons are not original. I have borrowed bits and pieces from many sources. In turn, I would hope that these bits and pieces will help others as they have helped me.

Sermons to Help Birth
the Interim Process

Sermon Title: "Joy Is Our Strength"
Texts: Nehemiah 8:10; John 15:11; 16:22

Church members need to feel positive about themselves. They need encouragement to face the unexpected things in life. I attempted in this message to encourage the church and remind it that Christian joy is our strength (Nehemiah 8:10); that Christian joy motivates us (John 15:11); and that Christians are not swept off their "joy feet" by circumstances.

I have learned to appreciate greatly three verses of scripture. Nehemiah 8:10 states, "The joy of the Lord is our strength." Then in John 15:11, it reads, "These things have I spoken unto you, that my joy might be in you, and that your joy might be full." And the third passage is found in John as well in the 16th chapter and the 22nd verse which reads, "And your joy no man taketh from you."

These verses have changed my approach to life. It occurred to me one day through these verses that God wanted me to be happy. It also occurred to me that I did not know what real joy was. So may I attempt to share with you some of the discoveries I have made regarding joy.

Some individuals have confused joy with a type of excitement. For example, some may think joy is that stomach-rolling feeling that they experience when they take that second dip on the roller coaster. Or for others it is like that surprised feeling the seventh grader had when he looked at his report card at the end of the school year and said, "My Lord, I passed!" Or for others it could be that leaping-in-the-air and clicking-the-heels-together feeling because they own a Toyota. And still for others it may be the excitement of being asked for a date. And for others joy might be the excitement of looking in the mirror and adjusting that first toupee. And could we not stretch the point and say some look on joy as that "thank goodness it's Friday" feeling.

The joy I wish to share is not a shallow type of emotional fling, but a solid experience of lasting strength. It is a joy that cannot be confined by bars or diminished with time. Nor can it be hidden in a crowd or changed by circumstances. This joy is one that is not weakened by criticism or destroyed by hate. This joy sings in the rain of disappointment and sees in the darkness of suffering. This joy believes in spite of the odds and lives by faith, hope, and love. It counts its blessings, not its problems, and hurts when others hurt. This joy reminds us who we are when we become discouraged and rallies us when we become weak.

Paul constantly reminded the early church to keep and guard this joy. His reason for this was because he knew the strength of joy. He knew it would give them that driving force they would need to face the obstacles ahead. So when he wrote to the Philippians he said that joy was a vital ingredient of the Christian's life (Philippians 1:3-4). When he wrote to the Thessalonians, he said to rejoice always as if it were the standing orders of the Christian (Thessalonians 5:16). When he wrote to the Colossians, he made joy the sustainer of every virtue and all knowledge (Colossians 1:9-11). When he wrote to the Romans, he said, "The Kingdom of heaven is righteousness and peace and joy" (Romans 14:17). Paul knew the strength and motivation of joy.

Jesus said it a little differently in John 15:11. He said, "I want you to have the joy that I have." It is interesting when Jesus said this. His earthly ministry was almost over. The little town around the Sea of Galilee had not repented even though His miracles had been seen. The Pharisees rejected Him and the Sadducees hated Him. No rabbi had joined Him and no scribe had sat at His feet. One disciple had betrayed Him and another would soon deny Him. With the beating and crucifixion only hours away, Jesus said to His disciples, "I want you to have the joy that I have." Jesus, like Paul, was encouraging the necessity of joy in these words, but the timing helps us to understand where joy receives its strength. Jesus was saying, "Even where I stand now, I have joy, and I want you to experience it also."

Now His joy was more than that of a brave man with a Christ-like mood. Jesus' joy was more than the sensation of being religiously busy. Jesus' joy was more than an emotional fling that would leave when the church lights were cut off. Jesus' joy was more than the pleasure that comes when one gives to the poor. Jesus' joy was that inner satisfaction and peace and victory that comes when one is in God's will. That was something "that no one could take away" (John 16:22).

Jesus wanted his followers to have that joy because He knew that it could not be destroyed and because it was the enduring and driving force of the Christian.

Jesus knew that without joy churches would be nothing more than spiritual convalescent homes. He knew that without joy pulpits would be dry, boring, and irreverent. Jesus knew that without joy Christians would not grow in the faith. Jesus knew that without joy church members would be fault finders instead of soul seekers. Jesus knew that without joy witnessing for Him would be a burden rather than an opportunity.

So Jesus wanted us to have that joy that comes when we allow God's will to control our lives.

I would not press the point, but I like to believe that Jesus is saying there is more to this joy than the satisfaction and victory and peace that come by being in God's will. Because He goes on to say in John 15:11, "And I want your joy to be full." It could be that He was saying, "There are some extra joys that I want you to have as well. In other words, there are some supplements of joy that I want you to experience."

For example, there is the joy of fellowship with other Christians, be it in church worship or in the home or hospital or wherever. There is joy in singing the hymns of praise; there is joy when other Christians invite us into their homes; there is joy when we bear one another's burdens.

And then there is the joy of the gospel, the joy of discovering it as Nicodemus did. And the joy of receiving the gospel as Zacchaeus did. And the joy of applying the gospel as the woman did who gave her few coins, which was all that she had.

I recall an experience that Gordon Bayless shared once. He said a lady came to his study and requested his counsel. She said, "You must tell me what to do. There is a lady in our church whom I do not get along with. She and I have not spoken to each other in over ten years, and I cannot continue like this. It is eating me up inside." Dr. Bayless turned to Matthew 5:23-24 and read to her and explained that it appeared according to the Bible that she needed to go to this lady and ask forgiveness. In these verses it plainly states that our worship and relationship to God are not valid until we are in a right relationship with our fellow man. "But," the lady replied, "it was her fault." "Nevertheless," Dr. Bayless said, "it says you are supposed to go to her." So the lady finally agreed to give it a try. Later that afternoon the lady returned to Dr. Bayless' study and said, "I had to come by and tell you what happened. I knocked on that lady's door and she came to the door and just cracked the door enough to see who I was and said, 'What do you want?' I asked her if I could come in. She then reluctantly opened the door a little wider and I turned sideways and went in. I sat on one end of the couch and she sat on the other. I began to tell her that I had come to apologize and that I was sorry that we had not been speaking to each other. The lady said, 'No, it was not your fault; it was mine!' And I said, 'No, it was mine.' And you know we almost had another disagreement, but we finally agreed that it was the fault of both of us. We agreed that both of us had been childish. And then we knelt down by the couch and prayed that God would forgive us for acting as we had. Then we got up and hugged one another and, Dr. Bayless, I had to come and tell you how good I feel now. I have not had this much joy in my heart in many, many years!" So there is a joy in applying the gospel to daily life and its conflicts.

Also there is a joy that comes when we experience the hand of God working in our lives. There is joy in knowing that He is there and that He walks with you as you raise your children, as you make decisions, as you experience the death of a relative or friend, as you risk your convictions and take a stand, and as you grow old. There is a joy in knowing that His hand is never shorter, that it always reaches out to help us along life's road.

Then there is that extra joy, that supplement of joy that we experience when we work in His Kingdom and witness in His world. I remember my first convert. She was a nine-year-old girl with red hair. She was beautiful that Sunday morning as she walked down the aisle of the little church where I was the pastor. I also will never forget the fulfilling joy that came over me that lasted and lasted. Extra joy comes to us when we witness and help others to find Him.

And that supplement of joy keeps on and on. Think of the extra joy that comes through answered prayer, and the joy of seeing our children serving in the church, and the joy of being a part of the program of the church.

And from all the joy that God gives to us, at the same time He gives us strength.

Knowing then the importance of joy in our lives and the strength we receive from it, I make these suggestions:

First, don't be swept off your joy feet by circumstances. Paul was in prison when he wrote the letter to the Philippians that has so much in it about joy. Jesus was soon to go to the cross and die when He told the disciples that He wanted them to have the joy that He had. When I think of circumstances interfering with our joy, I think of Grandma Wilhite. Early in her life she lost her husband in an accident. She raised their six children and sent them all to school and some of them to business school and college. She didn't remarry until after all the children had left home and were on their own. She was faithful to her church. One day I visited her and found that she and several other ladies were quilting quilts to make money to put a roof on the church. A short time after that, she and her husband were in an automobile accident that killed him and seriously injured her. Just before the accident, one of her sons who was a policeman was killed by bandits. Shortly after that another son was killed in an automobile accident. When she was in her late 80's I visited her in a rest home. She could still get about on her own. Where did I find her but down the hall helping some "old ladies" (as she called them) who could not do for themselves. She did not allow circumstances to destroy the joy that comes when we do our best to do God's will whatever life may bring.

Second, I encourage you to risk your joy. Don't be afraid to tell your neighbor or a relative or friend what brings you joy. When someone says, "How do you do it?" tell them. Don't try to claim all the credit. Tell them where your strength lies. Risk your joy. "The joy of the Lord is our strength." (Nehemiah 8:10)

And then I would encourage you to keep your joy revived. That is to say, work at it. God gives it to us, but we have to keep it alive. There is a beautiful example of this found in the story of the fifteen-year-old boy who was beginning to think through some of his spiritual feelings and questions. One Sunday morning during the invitation time, he went forward and told the pastor that he wanted his name taken off the church roll because he didn't feel the joy and excitement that he once did. The pastor asked the young fellow to meet him after the service in his study so they could discuss the matter. The young fellow agreed. As they entered the study, the pastor said that he would have to postpone their discussion until that night because he had a funeral that was quite a distance away and he would need to leave at once to make it on time. The young man agreed to wait and started out of the study when the pastor stopped him and said, "Don't you live on Oak Street?" The young man said, "Yes, why?" The pastor said, "There is an elderly man who lives on Oak Street who cannot come to church any more. He is old and can't walk or see to read. So I go by each Sunday afternoon and read a few verses of scripture with him and have prayer. Would you stop by and tell him that I couldn't come because of the funeral and while you are there read some scripture and have prayer with him?" The young man reluctantly said that he would. And the pastor said, "Come back tonight and we will talk about your wanting your name taken off the church roll." That night as the young man entered the pastor's study, the pastor said, "Now about taking your name off the church roll." The young man interrupted and said, "Pastor, let me tell you what happened to me this afternoon. I went over to that old man's house and told him what you said. Then I picked up his Bible and said, `The pastor asked me to read a few verses and have prayer.' The old man's eyes lit up and he said, `Good.' I read a few verses and then I said, `Let us pray,' but the old man said, `Read some more.' I read some more and said, `Let's pray,' but the old man wanted me to read some more. Every time I tried to stop reading and have prayer, the old man would say, `Read some more, son, read some more.' Now, pastor, about taking my name off the church roll, don't do that. Just give me the name of another old man to visit next Sunday because what happened to me today revived something within me, and I think that is what I need." So I encourage you to keep your joy revived.

Have you kept your joy revived? You will know. The strength of the church depends on the strength of its members.

Sermon Title: "Drops of Love"
Text: 1 Corinthians 13

*From time to time the church needs to take a fresh look at love.
Jesus said, "They shall know who you are because of your
love relationship." My hope for this sermon is that it might
encourage the church to operate on the level of Christian love.
My feeling is that the church struggles at this point. The
instinctive level, or customary level, of living is a rut in which
the church feels comfortable, causing it to drift away from the
Christian love level.*

Kathryn Booth was the daughter of William Booth, and
William Booth—as you know—was the man who established
the Salvation Army in 1878. Kathryn Booth followed in the
steps of her father and was a very dedicated person, working
with lost people, the down-and-out in the city, and the hungry.
When she died in 1955, her body was taken to Congress Hall in
London, England. Now the poor people of London claimed
Kathryn Booth. She had helped so many of them that they
thought she was theirs both alive and dead. But the government
of England thought that she was theirs because she had done so
much for England, especially for London. So both groups
gathered in large numbers for a last view of the body of Kathryn
Booth. Hungry, half-starved children were lined up on the street
along with the Ministers of Parliament to go in and view the
body of Kathryn Booth. I once read an account of her life that
reported that winos came by the casket and looked over into the
face of Kathryn Booth and burst into tears. Prostitute girls came

by the casket and turned away to beg people to take them home and help them to start new lives. A drunkard came by and said, "That woman lived for me." Someone caught him by the arm and led him to the side. In a few moments he was on his knees and said, "From this day on, her God is going to be my God as long as I live." Three men knelt at the head of the casket of Kathryn Booth, and all three of them confessed their sins, and all three of them left Congress Hall that day saved. A man said, "I came 60 miles to see this woman for the last time because she is responsible for saving my three sons from a wasted life." Isn't it wonderful to have such a testimony as Kathryn Booth? She had a testimony of love that brought men and women to repentance even as her body was lying there in a casket in Congress Hall. What a testimony! I ask you this question: "What has happened to that love? What has happened to the love that Kathryn Booth had?" My conviction is that today we are trying to operate on as little love as we possibly can. The juvenile problems in this country are existing because we are trying to get by with as little parental love as we possibly can. The divorce problem that exists in our land is largely because we are trying to get by with as little companion love as possible. The social and racial problems that still haunt us constantly exist because we have tried to get by with as little neighborly love as possible. National and international conflicts exist in our world today because nation after nation is trying to get by with as little of God's love as possible.

There is a story told of a woman in the New Testament, one of the most beautiful stories in the entire Bible. This woman was in Bethany. While Jesus was in the house of Simon, this woman came with a jar or a box - the Scripture says an alabaster box - of precious perfume, probably a little clay jar of some kind. She brought the jar and broke it and poured the contents on the feet of Jesus and wiped His feet with her hair. She was rebuked and told this could be sold and given to the poor. Jesus said, "Leave her alone. She has done what she could. She came beforehand to anoint my body for burial." The point in the story for me is this: She did not pour just a little drop on the feet of Jesus. Nor did she pour two or three drops, but she broke the box and poured the entire contents. We are trying to operate off drops. Drops of love will not suffice. Drops of love will not suffice in the forgiving process. Drops of love will not revive our spirits. When Jesus said, "Love thy neighbor as thyself," it was not with a drop, but to love your neighbor with all you know how, with all that you are, wishing the best for him or her.

There are many people who do not understand love, and there are many people who do not know how to love. There are some who are frustrated about love. One of the first things that I noticed as a prison chaplain was that many of the inmates had tattoos. Some had tattoos on their fingers. Some had L O V E tattooed on the fingers of one hand and H A T E tattooed on the fingers of the other hand. I don't know what that said to them, but to me it said, "I am confused." "I don't know how to understand these two things." They might have been saying, "Someone has abused me." "I've never been taught to love." "I've known only hate." "Oh, if I could only know love!" I know people are confused about love. I know of a woman who said she loved her husband very dearly, but her husband told me that she caught him asleep on the couch one day and beat him over the head with a hardback Bible.

I think it is easy to confuse love with other things - for example, lust. There are times when one may say, "I love you," but a real honest to goodness expression would be, "I lust you or lust what you have that I might benefit from." We confuse love with lust. We confuse love with concern. We see some-body in need and call the welfare department and say, "Would you go down to such and such address? They are in need." That's not what Jesus said when he gave us the story of the good Samaritan. He told us that the Samaritan got in the ditch and helped. Jesus is saying in that story that every individual is a welfare department. Also, we many times confuse love with goodness. In a hotel where I stayed one night, there was a card on the table that read, "Love is leaving the towels in this room." We can be good little boys. We can be religiously busy and we can be morally good, but we can be cold when it comes to love. We confuse love and goodness. We confuse love and emotion. Embracing, handshaking, weeping, and such do not necessarily mean that one loves.

We might better understand love if we had a better usage of words to describe our feelings. The Greeks had three different words for love. When they wanted to refer to a friend, they had a word that they used. When they wanted to refer to their love for their family or their country, they had another word they used. When they wanted to refer to love for the opposite sex, such as a wife or sweetheart, they had another word they used. Then Jesus came along. Jesus said these words were not adequate to express the love that a Christian ought to have for another. He coined a new word, "agape." Agape means unconditional love, a love without any strings attached to it. It means that God will never seek anything that would hurt or harm an individual. It means in turn that I would not seek that which will hurt or destroy or put the other person down. It's unconditional love. It's love regardless of what a person looks like or what a person's habits are. It's love in the very highest degree possible.

Maybe we don't understand love because we have just one little word, "L O V E," in the English language to express love. We handle it so loosely. We just throw that word around any place. I've been reading bumper stickers lately. One bumper sticker said, "Atlanta is a love city." That one needs some explaining. Another one I saw read, "I love Clayton County." I saw another one that said, "I love my Volvo." Another said, "I love my parakeet." You see, we use the same little word to say, "I love cornbread," as we do to say, "Oh, how I love Jesus." One of the problems is that we are limited in expressing ourselves. How we understand love might depend on how we have been able to express it and to define it.

I think the Apostle Paul helped us a lot when he shared in the letter to the Corinthians not a definition of love, but rather some results or characteristics of love. He is saying that love is the act of the total individual. When a person says to me, "I've fallen in love with Jane," that's something he couldn't help. That's right; he couldn't help it. His emotions have driven him. His eyes were attracted to her. He liked her personality. He fell in love with her. When Paul talks about love, it is more than just the emotion. It is the total being. Paul is saying here that it takes all that an individual is. It takes his mind and his spirit and his heart all together. This love involves the total individual. It is not some emotional fling. Paul goes on to say in the last few verses of this chapter, "When I was a child, my speech and feeling and thinking were those of a child. Now that I am a man, I have no more use for childish ways. What we see now is like a dim image in a mirror. Then we shall see face to face. What I know now is partial; then it will be complete, as complete as God's knowledge of me. Meanwhile, these three: faith, hope and love, and the greatest of these is love." I think we need to turn back and read one more time this verse, "When I was a child, my feelings and thinking were those of a child; now that I am a man, I have put away childish things." Paul is saying here that we can measure our love by our maturity. He says, "When I was not saved, I acted like a child. Now that I have been saved, I act differently." Paul is saying the new birth has brought a new level of maturity.

I walked past the desk of a secretary who had framed a little article on maturity that caught my eye. Here are some of the things it said. Maturity is the ability to handle frustration, control anger, and settle differences. Maturity is patient. Maturity is sweating out a situation in spite of opposition and setbacks. Maturity is responding to the needs of others. Maturity is the ability to face unpleasantness and disappointment without becoming bitter. Maturity is the gift of remaining calm. It is the ability to disagree without being disagreeable. Maturity is humility. Maturity is the ability to make a decision, to act on that decision, and to accept full responsibility of the outcome. Maturity means dependability, integrity, keeping one's word. Maturity is the ability to live in peace with that which we cannot change. I think Paul is saying this about love: when I grew up and became a Christian, I no longer acted like a child.

I have a recording that tells about the various conflicts in home life. One of the conflicts is the problem between brothers and sisters. It tells about a little girl who got into an argument with her brother, and she decided to run to her daddy. She ran into the house and found her daddy in his chair in the den. She hopped in his lap and put her arms around his neck, and he put his arms around her. Now she was safe and secure from her brother. All of a sudden as she is looking over her dad's shoulder with their arms around each other, her brother comes in. As he comes straight toward her, she feels that security of her father and sticks her tongue out at her brother. A lot of times that describes where we are. So many times we say, "I love God," and then stick our tongues out at our brothers. It's very difficult for us to really say we love God when we cannot get along and love those about us. The Scripture says, "How can I love God whom I have not seen and not love my brother whom I have seen?" I believe we can easily measure our love for God by how we stand with our brother. We know how much we love God by the love that we have for our fellow man. How much do we love God? How much do we love our fellow man?

John had something to say about that, and I want to read this passage to you. He said, "Dear friends, let us love one another for love comes from God. Whoever loves is a child of God and knows God. Whoever does not love does not know God because God is love. This is how God shows His love for us. He sent his only Son into the world that we might have life through Him. This is what love is. It is not that we have loved God, but that

He has loved us and sent his Son to be the means by which our sins are forgiven. Dear friends, if this is how God loves us, then we should love one another. No one has ever seen God. If we love one another, God lives in us. His love is made perfect within us. We love because God first loved us. If any man says, 'I love God,' and hates his brother, he is a liar for he cannot love God whom he has not seen if he does not love his brother whom he has seen. This then is the commandment that Christ gave us—he who loves God must love his brother also."

Love is the content we must have if God is to bless his people. If the Holy Spirit is to come and help us, we must love one another. I encourage you to start a campaign today, your own personal campaign that you are going to love everybody, that you are going to practice what God's Word says. First we are to love Him, and then we are to love; agape love, Christian love, not love like a friend, not love like the opposite sex, not love like patriotism for our country, but love that keeps on keeping on, and love that helps us to understand, and love that helps us to forgive regardless of what that individual might look like or what that individual might have said. You see, it is only love that can bring the answer to any church or to any life. I encourage you to season your life and this church and this community with love.

When I was a boy coming up, one of my jobs was to bring in little chips of wood called kindling. The kindling was not to produce heat for the room. You don't use kindling to heat a room; you use kindling to get a back log to burn. God is depending on us to provide the kindling of love so He can do His work. It is the kindling of our love that God depends on.

"Love one another," he said. When that kindling gets the back log of God's Spirit and God's love working in this church and in this community, things are going to happen. We have to love. It is only love that breaks down the wall of pride. It is only love that brings new life to our church and to our homes. It is only love that melts the coldest heart. It is only love that bears more sorrow. It is only love that stops the gossiper's tongue. Only love endures more hardship. Only love understands young people. Only love can be patient with the drunkard. Only love can forgive and forget. Only love can serve without rewards. It is only love that goes beyond the call of duty and only love that steps out on faith. Jesus said, "They shall know that ye are my disciples because ye love one another."

The first passage that I learned as a child was this: God is love. It took me a long time before I understood the meaning of it. The meaning is simply this: God is love. Not love is God. Do you see what it is saying? It says that in order to have love, I must have God. So many times we are trying to get the love before we get God. I'm saying that in order to have the Christian agape love I have been talking about, we must have God in our hearts. That is really what happens when you trust Him as your Savior and Lord. He puts a pinch of His love in your heart. You are not the same from then on. The passage that really describes that is John 3:16, "For God so loved the world that he gave his only Son that whosoever believes in him shall not perish but have everlasting life." Do you have that love? Do you have the love that can forgive and forget? Do you have the love that causes you to love other people regardless? Do you have the love that would cause you to move the fence out a little further?

From the Second World War comes a story about two soldiers who discovered their friend had been shot by a sniper. They decided they would find a place to bury him other than in the woods. They took the body to a little Catholic chapel that had a cemetery beside it. They went to the chapel and asked the priest if they could bury their friend in the church cemetery. The priest asked, "Is he Catholic?" They answered, "No, he is not." The priest said, "I am sorry; we don't allow anyone but Catholics to be buried in this cemetery." The two soldiers were very disappointed. They asked the priest, "Is there any harm in burying him just outside the cemetery fence?" The priest said, "No," so they buried him just outside the fence. The next morning they wanted to go by once more to see the grave where they had buried their friend. They could not find the grave. They could not find the fresh dirt. They looked and they looked. Finally, they looked over the stone fence, and there they saw the grave in the cemetery. During the night the priest had rearranged the stone fence so that it would include the grave of their soldier friend.

What is love? Love is rearranging the fence so that it takes in people and loves them and forgives them and understands them and is patient with them. God help us to have that love so we can move our fence.

Sermons to Help Stabilize the Church

Sermon Title: "The Struggling Church in Today's World"
Text: Matthew 16:18; 2 Corinthians 5:14-21; 6:1

The church has always struggled and will continue to do so.
This sermon is an attempt to call attention to this fact and offer
comfort as well as challenge. Hopefully it will encourage the
church to evaluate its goals and plans for the future.

My first memories of the church go back to Christmas time
when on Christmas Eve we would go to church for a worship
service. The children presented the story of the birth of Jesus.
Then every child was given a gift from his teacher and a paper
bag containing an apple and orange and some candy.

Then I remember the church in my growing-up years when
on Mother's Day there were two tubs in the foyer of the church
filled with white and red roses. As we entered the church we
selected a rose and pinned it on to honor our mother, red if she
was living and white if she was not living.

I remember Easter when I wore a starched white shirt and
white pants. I remember Vacation Bible School and being
introduced to my first "Kool Aid." I remember Bible drill and
B.Y.P.U. and RAs. I remember the church catching on fire. I
remember the old pump organ and Mrs. Farley who played it.
I remember being baptized. I remember my pastors, Brother
Rushing who led me to Christ, and Brother Bandy, and Brother
Davis. I remember the church ordaining me to preach. Through

the years the church has taught me many things:

- ■The church has taught me about Jesus Christ and that He died to pay the sin debt of mankind.
- ■The church has taught me about the Bible and faith and prayer.
- ■The church has taught me to appreciate all the good things that have been showered upon me.
- ■The church has helped me to find peace and contentment.
- ■The church has given me friends.

But another thing that I remember about the church is that it has always struggled. As long as I can remember the church has struggled.

- ■It has struggled to keep in step with the times.
- ■It has struggled to be true to its mission.
- ■It has struggled to find answers to questions regarding sin, afterlife, divorce, abortion, capital punishment, alcoholism, and missions.
- ■It has struggled to pay its bills and keep its members.
- ■It has struggled with doctrine and authority.

The church has always struggled and will continue to do so; however, it must be said over and over again that each generation must take afresh its responsibility of the struggling church.

I am sure of three things as I experience the struggling church in my life and the Bible. First, struggle as it will, "the gates of hell," the world, the unconcerned majority, "will not destroy the church." Second, I am just as sure that the message of the church will not change. The message of the church is "ye must be born again." We can change the architecture of the church. We can change its name. We can call it high church or low church. We can even classify it in denominations and even divide the denominations into fundamentalists and moderates, but its message will never change.

Also, I am certain that the responsibility of the church will not be withdrawn. If I understand Matthew 28:19-20, it says that "we are to go and teach all nations." Then He promises that He "will be with us to the end of the age." To me this means that this responsibility will not be completed until He returns.

When Paul wrote his letters to the Corinthian Church, it was struggling. A close reading of First and Second Corinthians causes one to wonder how those early Christians continued. No doubt, Paul's letters gave them comfort and guidance which they needed so badly.

I am reminded of II Corinthians 5:14-21; 6:1 because it is in these passages that Paul reminds the church of several basic things that the church must remember as it struggles from day to day. I want to share these with you because we are no different than that early church, and these give us guidance and comfort as well.

First he said in verses 18 and 19 that the church must take the ministry of reconciliation seriously. "Reconcile" means to restore a lost relationship. The work of Christ on the cross was to restore a right relationship between man and God. Through man's disobedience and rebellion toward God, the relationship was broken, and God provided a way to restore that broken relationship which is called reconciliation.

I sat on the front porch with a man once who pointed down the road to a house and said, "My son lives yonder in that house, but he has not spoken to me or his mother in over ten years." Then he said, "Oh, I wish we could be reconciled." There are many people on the outs with God; that is they don't pray to Him, they don't read His Word, they don't worship Him. And you see these are most important because

- ▪Prayer keeps us in touch with God.
- ▪Bible reading helps us to understand how God relates to us.
- ▪And worship is that fellowship with God's family where we find support, love, and courage and where we dedicate ourselves to Him.

These are most important because without them we drift away from God. Paul is saying to the church that our task is to participate in the ministry of reconciliation, to bring people to a right relationship with God.

- ▪In a land where honesty has become what you can get by with, we need to reconcile men to God.
- ▪In a society where "if two people sleep together," it's called a home, we need to reconcile men to God.
- ▪In our cities where old women are being raped and killed and where more children are abused than ever before in history, we need to reconcile men to God.
- ▪In a land where Bible reading is old-fashioned and church going is sissy; where the pulpit is ruled by politics; where people have to be begged to worship; and where people

think they are as good as they need to be, we need to
reconcile men to God.

■In our churches where we spend more time talking about
ministry than we spend time actually doing ministry, we
need to reconcile men to God. Let us never lose sight of
our task as a struggling church and that is to be a part of
the reconciling process with God.

The second thing that Paul reminds us about in these verses
is that the church must take conversion to mean that one has
changed. If I know anything about the business world, it is this:
most people will buy a cheaper product if it looks the same as
a higher priced one. Now, when people see no difference in a
church member; if his life is no cleaner, no purer; if he does not
live a more righteous life; then I assure you they are not going
to spend money and time to come to Christ or the church.
People are not coming to Christ until they see something better,
until we live like Christ!

■The day has come when we can no longer hide behind a
creed or a denomination or a tradition, or our doctrine. The
world is saying, "If you have it, live it."

■The day has come when we can build our steeples no taller;
the day has come when we cannot impress the masses with
our showmanship; the day has come when our plush
building will not suffice; the day has come when we can
no longer brag about our schools and degrees. The day has
come when those on the outside are saying, "If you have
it, live it!"

■The day has come when the pastor of the church must stand

the test as a shepherd of the flock. To love people as Christ loved people - that is the test of the pastor today. The day has come when the people are saying, "Pastor, if you preach it, live it."

■The day has come when sin is being redefined and a spade is being called a spade, and the world is saying to the church, "Tell it like it is and live it!"

The church must take conversion to mean that one has changed.

During my college days, I was pastor of a little church up in Tennessee. There was a man who would never come to church except during revival when he would come and stay outside and listen to the worship service. One day I got a call that his wife, who was a faithful member of the church, had died unexpectedly. I went for the funeral and then by his home before I headed back to college. He asked me if I would spend the night with him, and I did. Before we retired that night, I asked him to join me for a scripture reading and prayer. After the prayer, I noticed he was crying. I asked him about his relationship to God. He indicated that he wanted to repent and trust in God as his Savior and Lord. Then he started coming to Sunday church services and Wednesday prayer meeting. He never missed. He did this for a whole year, but would not join the church. Finally after a year he came forward and joined the church. I asked him afterward why he waited so long. He said, "I wanted the people to know that I meant business and that I was really converted."

The struggling church today must teach and live what Paul said to Corinth in verse 17, "Therefore, if any man be in Christ, he is a new creature. Old things are passed away; behold, all things are become new."

Paul also encouraged the struggling church not to lose its joy. Look at verse 14 where he says, "We are ruled by the love of Christ." There is joy in that. But when he wrote in Philippians 1:3 and 4 to the struggling church at Philippi, he called on them to recover their joy because it was the vital ingredient of the Christian life. When he wrote in First Thessalonians 5:16 to the struggling church, he said, "Rejoice always," as if it were the standing orders of the Christian.

And when he wrote in Colossians 1:9-11, he said to the struggling church at Colossae, "Joy is the sustainer of every virtue and all knowledge." Sustainer means "strength" - the strength of your church lies in your joy.

And when Paul wrote to the struggling church at Rome, he said, "The Kingdom of heaven is righteousness and peace and joy."

In each case Paul is informing the struggling churches that the church loses its joy when claims attack the church. Paul is saying that the church is a family; it is a household of faith; it is the living Temple of God; it is the body of Christ; it is the bride of Christ; and no one can lay claim on it.

- ■The church does not belong to the pastor, the deacons, the trustees, the music department, the educational department; it doesn't belong to the Women's Missionary Union, or the youth; it doesn't even belong to the congregation.
- ■Ultimately the church belongs to Christ, and for someone or some group to try to claim it destroys the joy of the

church.

The church must not lose that joy of

- ■answered prayer,
- ■of hearing Christ being preached,
- ■of having fellowship with others, and
- ■seeing others turn to God in repentance and faith.

It needs to be said at this point that it is very clear why youth are not staying in the church when they hit the teens. It is because youth will simply not stay around where there is no joy.

Paul seems to have one other suggestion for the church at Corinth and certainly for the struggling churches of today, and that is verses 20 and 21 and in chapter 6, verse 1.

As I understand it, Paul is saying that the church, in spite of its struggling, should never lose sight of its task to witness.

Many have confused the task of the church. They see the building as the place to witness, but this is not what it was intended to be.

The church is the empowering and the equipping base and not the base of operations.

The church is a community of believers scattered out into homes, shops, factories, offices, schools, and recreational centers—but it is still the church.

What we do when we are scattered is the test of the quality of what we do when we are gathered. I am not too proud of my denomination at this point. We are spending more for interest on borrowed money to build beautiful buildings for worship than we spend on both home and foreign missions combined.

We are "ambassadors" which means we go out to represent Christ in the marketplace, hospital, school, community, wherever we are scattered.

What the world needs so desperately today is the saving grace and love of Jesus Christ, and we as the struggling church must never lose sight of the fact that He has called us to represent Him out there where we live.

Today is no different than it was during Paul's day, and this church is no different than the rest. We all struggle. As we do so, let us not lower our standards or neglect our tasks. As we struggle, let us remember that "the joy of the Lord is our strength."

The day has come when the church must come alive with people like you and me scattered throughout our community living what we preach. We cannot box up the church in this building. We must live it out there. We cannot box it up in a little cassette tape. We must live it out there. Just recording it will not do. Just preaching it will not do. We must go out there where we meet people each day and live Christ before others.

In the church where I was interim pastor several years ago, I heard a musical entitled, "We Are the Church," and some of the words impressed me so that I want to share them with you.

> Jesus—the Son of God—stepped from eternity into time.
> Within him he carried a plan which has been laid before the foundation of the world.
> Jesus would establish the Kingdom of God on earth.
> This kingdom would not be built with bricks and mor-

tar—but with living stones.

So Jesus walked through Galilee and Judea calling people to follow him.

He had no organization, no buildings, no funds, no distinguished patrons, no membership forms. But he had good news. . . .

For ordinary people who gathered around Jesus became extraordinary; from fishermen and physicians, tax men and harlots he formed his new creation - the company of the forgiven and regenerated - a marvel and an astonishment in the eyes of the old creation.

They would live after he died. They would rise up after he arose. He would ascend but those first disciples would remain as the firstborn among many brethren. They were the church of yesterday. We are the church of today.

Lord Jesus, you are the foundation of the church and of this congregation.

Unite our hearts and minds in this place and send your Spirit to us, your waiting disciples.

Give us a vision of your church that is great enough to transform our battered, broken world.

Lord, we have known your glory and we will never be the same. But will the world be any different because we have spent this time in your presence? Help us take the glory that has filled this room and move out through a world that is hungry and hostile and hurting. Help us to be a sanctuary for those who have not seen your glory. Together, with your power, *we can, we must* change this world.

Amen.

Sermon Title: "The Church Reclaiming the Holy Spirit"
Text: John 14:15-17; Acts 1:4-8

The purpose of this sermon during the interim time is to direct the church back to its source of help and strength. It is to encourage the church to allow the Holy Spirit to work in individuals and in the life of the church. Hopefully, this sermon will also provide a better working understanding of and commitment to the Holy Spirit.

A little group of about 120 made up the beginning of the first church. They were poor, plain, simple folks. To this little group, Jesus had given the task of witnessing unto those in Jerusalem, Judea, Samaria, and the ends of the earth. The task seemed impossible, and it was without help. So Jesus told this little group of about 120 to "wait" (Acts 1:4-8). "Wait" for what? "Wait" for the power to help them do their task. They waited and that power did come. With little organization and resources, this little group in 30 years had reached Rome and numbered over 100,000 converts! The only way this miracle can be explained is to realize that those early Christians had received a power, a power to help them do their task.

Today our church needs this power. We have a task to do. We must find a pastor; and if we find the pastor God wants us to have here, we must have the help of the Holy Spirit in this place. We must provide a witness in this community; and if we continue to minister to the youth, to newcomers, to the aging, to the sick, to the forgotten and the lost and unchurched, we must have a source to help us, that being the strength and power of the Holy Spirit.

If the church reclaims the help of the Holy Spirit, I think we must begin with two very basic questions. First: What is the Holy Spirit, and how does it work? Second: Why is the Holy Spirit so desperately needed?

Many words have been used to describe the nature and working of the Holy Spirit. The apostle John called the Holy Spirit "water" because it brings refreshment and cleansing like water. John the Baptist used the word "fire" to describe the Holy Spirit because it gives light and searches out like fire. Jesus called the Holy Spirit "oil" because of the healing and comfort that oil brings. Luke called it "wind" because of its powerful but invisible effect. Matthew described the Holy Spirit as being like a "dove" because of its meekness and forgiveness as symbolized in a dove. Paul explained the Holy Spirit as a "voice" because it speaks and warns like a voice. When John wrote the Revelation, he used the word "seal" to characterize the Holy Spirit. A seal meant security, and to him the Holy Spirit brought security.

Not only are there words that describe and define the Holy Spirit, but there are the activities of the Holy Spirit that deepen our understanding as well. For example, in John's Gospel it is stated that the Holy Spirit "dwells with us and teaches us," that it "brings to remembrance," it "bears witness," it "convinces of sin," it "guides" and "speaks" and "declares." In the book of Acts, the writer states that the Holy Spirit is a "power" or "influence" and a "person." Also, that it "inspires the scripture" and "speaks through them." It "calls ministers," "sends out workers," and "forbids certain actions." And finally in the book of Romans we find statements indicating that the Holy Spirit "intercedes" and has a "mind," a "will," and a "personality." All to say, that the Holy Spirit is active.

Even with all the above descriptive terms, the Holy Spirit is not fully explained. The Greeks tried to explain it further by using the word *parakletos* which means "someone who is called out." They used *parakletos* to identify one who was called to court to witness in another's behalf or to give expert advice. Also it was used at times to identify one called to give encouragement. So this same word was used to describe the Holy Spirit.

Maybe another way of understanding the Holy Spirit is to see it as a person who helps us cope with life. It helps us to look at life squarely in the eye and does not play games. It is always there to help us cope with life. It gives us common sense as we face decisions. It gives us courage to keep hanging on. It gives us wisdom to know what is best. It gives us insight to know right from wrong. In short, the Holy Spirit comes to take away our inadequacies and provides us with an insight to see and cope with life. For example, a doctor can look at a human body and see more than the average person. An artist can see more in a painting than a person who cannot paint. The Holy Spirit is that extra insight that the Christian has that helps him interpret life. It is that help which equips one's life to take on real meaning. Our church needs this insight, this coping assistance, that the Holy Spirit gives if we find God's will in the days that lie ahead.

This brings us to our second question: Why does the church

so desperately need the Holy Spirit? For one thing, it puts life into the message of the church. I am fascinated by seed. I can plant a little seed, knowing that it has something that I cannot even see, and that is life. But it is there. Because after a while a new stalk comes up! The message of the church must have the Holy Spirit because it is the life of the message. Without this Holy Spirit life, the pulpit becomes a place of steam blowing, opinions, doubt, and personal glamour. Only the Holy Spirit can save preaching.

Also, the church needs the Holy Spirit because it is the source that completes the redemption process. God our heavenly Father loved us, and His only begotten Son died for us, and it is the Holy Spirit that convicts our hearts and converts us to a new life.

So the church needs the Holy Spirit because it is the Holy Spirit that reveals God's truth to us personally.

The Holy Spirit is important to the church also because there can be no real growth in faith without it. Take the Bible for example; without the Holy Spirit, it is only paper and ink. It was the spirit of God that moved men to write the Bible, and it is the same spirit that relays that message to you and me when we read it. The Bible comes alive through the Holy Spirit. Its truth convicts us. Its simplicity calls us. Its power sends us out to witness. And it is through the Holy Spirit and our reading of the Bible that we grow in faith.

It is the Holy Spirit, as well, that keeps the fellowship of the church alive. It creates unity, concern for one another, and brotherly love. Likewise, worship loses its appeal and purpose without the Holy Spirit. Worship becomes "holy entertainment," a "show and tell," a "make believe game" without the Holy Spirit. Prayer, too, is dead without the Holy Spirit. It becomes a "daily exercise," a "thank you, Lord, that I am not as other men are," a "drive-in window where we place our spiritual orders" without the Holy Spirit.

So the Holy Spirit is the life-giving source that inspires us to understand His Word, that keeps the fellowship of the church alive, and is the strength of our prayers and worship; all of which helps us to grow in faith, hope, and love.

Let us be reminded also that without the Holy Spirit, the church will not be effective in its witnessing. At Pentecost 3,000 were converted and added to the church. This was because the Holy Spirit was there. The early church "added daily to the church such as was saved." This was because the Holy Spirit was there.

In his book entitled *How Firm a Foundation*, R. C. Campbell tells the account of a camp meeting in Clay County, North Carolina. He said the preachers in that area met to decide who would preach and when during the camp meeting. They were accustomed to having four services each day, one at 8:00 AM, another at 11:30 AM, another at 4:00 PM, and another at 7:00 PM. A preacher, Elijah Kimsey, spoke up and said he would like to speak at the 8:00 AM service. The next morning when the 8:00 AM service began, Elijah Kimsey stood and preached. Instead of stopping when his time was up, he just kept preaching right on through the 11:30 AM service. People began to see that the Holy Spirit was blessing the old mountain preacher. Many listeners began to leave and go out to find others and encourage them to come to the service. Elijah Kimsey preached right on through the 4:00 PM and 7:00 PM services and on into the night before he finally stopped. There were more than 500 people converted that day. It was said that this one service meant more to Southwest North Carolina, Northeast Georgia, and East Tennessee than anything that had ever happened in that part of the country. Records will reveal that thousands of churches in this country last year did not have a single convert the entire year.

I was in the airport in Boston once and saw a huge gadget encased in glass. It ran without an outside source of power. Wheels were turning, bells were ringing, and balls were rolling down tracks. It was very interesting to stand there and watch it run. As I watched, someone asked, "What does it do?" I overheard the reply, "It doesn't do anything; it just runs." This is what happens when a church tries to operate on its own power and without the outside source of the Holy Spirit. What does it do? It just runs. There is no growth in faith. There are no converts.

When God breathes into a church the life-giving power of the Holy Spirit, that church will not just run.

We can and must reclaim the Holy Spirit for our church. We do this by "presenting ourselves" (Romans 12:1) to God and "receiving" and "walking in Him" (Colossians 2:6). The old sailor made it clear when he said, "I don't understand the wind, but I do know how to hoist a sail." We may not know all that we would like to know about the Holy Spirit, but we can say as the sail depends on the wind for its strength, I will commit myself to the Holy Spirit for my strength and source to cope with life.

Sermons to Conclude the Interim Time

Sermon Title: "Getting Ready for a Pastor"
Text: Joshua 3:5

Preparation is most important. In this message I attempt to stress the importance of getting ready for the coming of a pastor. I point out that the entire membership is accountable and that the future will be hindered unless constructive preparation is made.

We spend a great deal of our time getting ready. The athlete spends months and years getting ready for one event. The professional person spends years in training getting ready to perform a certain task. We spend months and go to great expense for a wedding ceremony. All to say, getting ready for a pastor is important as well. If the Israelites wandered forty years in the wilderness because they were not ready to enter the promised land, it might be wise for us to make certain that we are ready for the coming of a new pastor. Not that the two are the same, but that preparation is essential.

Getting ready for a pastor requires some soul searching on our part. It requires taking a look at ourselves and our church. It requires commitment and vision.

Getting ready for a pastor requires that we look at the past and make certain that there is no unfinished business. First we make certain that all the former pastors have been released. I did not say forget them, but rather release them. This is not easy in many cases because they married our children, baptized our grandchildren, and stood by the grave when we buried our dead. But until we release the former pastors with appreciation for what they did, big or small, and for the foundations they might have laid for us to build on, we hinder the process that must take place if we get ready for a new pastor.

What takes place is simple. By not releasing the former pastor or pastors, we open ourselves to comparing any prospective pastor with former pastors. None will compare. What we need to acknowledge is that ministers are all different and each one can be used of God as God plans. We must not allow the fine ministry of our former pastors to hinder one that might be sent our way. We get ready for a pastor by releasing the former pastor or pastors. Some have said, "We will never get another pastor like the last one we had." That does not mean that God cannot lead us to one who can do the task that needs to be done in the life of our church.

We can also get ready for a pastor by making certain that our past mistakes and problems have been dealt with. A new pastor should not be asked to inherit our unresolved problems. I have worked with many churches that never attempted to resolve their life-long church problems. Instead, they just keep their problems on the back burner and every so often they pull them over on the front burner and turn up the heat. The pastor leaves because he is caught in the middle, and for several months the church battles over who has control. They never seem to resolve the issue; they just get tired of the battle so they back away (put it on the back burner again) and find another preacher and in a few years repeat the process.

We have no right to require that a new pastor inherit our problems. There is no better time than now (during the interim time) to abolish this hidden monster in the church. Maybe you need to go to someone in the church and say, "The past was not what it should have been;" "I was too hasty;" "I was stubborn;" "I wanted my way;" "Please forgive me;" "Let's lay this to rest forever;" "I do not want to stand in the way of our church and a new pastor." The church is no place to play games with one another's feelings and the effectiveness of the church.

This is one thing Jesus was dealing with in Matthew 5:21-24 when He said, "When you come to the altar and remember that your brother and yourself are not in a right relationship with one another, go first and make things right with your brother and then come and worship." We get ready for a pastor by being sure our pastor does not inherit our unresolved problems.

Important as well, as we get ready for a pastor, is that we establish some dreams and visions for our church. To state it another way, we need some goals and plans. A church will not grow beyond its goals and dreams and plans and visions. The prospective pastor will certainly ask your search committee what your church plans and goals are. You need to establish goals and plan how to reach those goals together as a church. This is what a prospective pastor will be looking for as he considers a change. He will ask himself, "Where is this church headed?" "Are they looking for a slave or a servant?" "Will I be challenged?" "Are they willing to risk in order to accomplish their goals?" In other words, the prospective pastor does not want to invest his life in a church that is not going someplace. Many churches have lost the possibility of acquiring excellent pastors because they simply didn't know where they were going; they had no goal and plans.

One other matter is quite clear also as the church gets ready for a pastor, and that has to do with our spiritual preparation. As the Israelites approached the bank of the Jordan River after forty years of preparation, Joshua said, "Sanctify yourselves for tomorrow I will do great wonders among you." Before God could use them in His plan they first had to prepare themselves spiritually. He called on them to sanctify themselves. In the Old Testament sanctification always meant two things: separation from sin and dedication to God. God waited until they were ready spiritually before they crossed the Jordan River to accomplish His plan. In Acts 2:1 we find Jesus telling the early church to "wait" (get ready) and there in the upper room they prayed until they were in one accord, until they were ready. In the garden, Jesus prayed and prepared Himself until He could say, "Not my will, but thine." The Apostle Paul prepared himself for a very difficult ministry by spending time in the wilderness. Isaiah went to the temple (Isaiah 6:8) and prepared himself spiritually until he could say, "Here am I; send me."

We get ready for God to use us and our pastor by preparing ourselves spiritually.

Maybe we need to say today that whatever it takes to get ready for a pastor, I want to do it:

- ■If it means making things right with my fellow man, I want to do it.
- ■If it means becoming involved in the plans and dreams of this church, I want to do it.

■If it means committing myself to prayer until my attitude is right, I want to do it.

Whatever it takes to get ready, are you willing?

Getting ready is important. Are you as an individual ready? Is the church ready for another pastor, or do we need to put the search committee on hold until we are ready?

Title: "Understanding and Working with Your Pastor"
Text: John 1:6-8

An interim pastor can tactfully share with the church at this point in the interim process very helpful information as well as suggestions. This could be the last sermon prior to the new pastor's coming.

In this sermon I have sought to deal with the specific role of the pastor and his effectiveness. The application is for the church to rally around the pastor with support and unity.

As you look forward to the arrival of your new pastor, it is not unusual that questions might float through your mind. There are healthy questions such as: What kind of person will the new pastor be? Will the two of us like each other? Can we expect the new minister to be a good pastor as well as a good speaker? Such questions are valid, and I would like to attempt in this message to lighten the stress and make it easier for you and the church as these questions surface.

Many pastors are leaving the pastorate because neither the pastor nor the church understands the pastor's calling or the task he is called to perform. Most ministers think they ought to be able to do everything that is asked or expected of them, and the church feels that the pastor is some type of superman and can do it.

John 1:6-8 provides us insight at this point. These verses are talking about John the Baptist, but they reflect an understanding that applies to all ministers. They focus on the three characteristics of a minister. First, he was a man with human limitations (verse 6). Second, he was a man sent from God (verse 6). And third, he came to bear witness (verse 7). Let us look at these a little closer.

"He was a man." Sometimes we forget that our pastor is a man with human limitations. He gets sick, tired, depressed, and angry. He doesn't get better gas mileage, his groceries cost the same, and he has to send his children to college too. His children are not perfect, and his wife is not superwoman.

I hear comments like these regarding ministers: "He is a good man, but. . . ." "He is a powerful preacher, but a poor pastor." "He works well with adults, but the youth don't like him." "He is a good Bible teacher, but not an evangelist." Such statements are made because many do not understand the nature and work of the pastor.

Why didn't God send some type of angelic being instead of a minister to look after the church? He chose a man with human limitations, a product of His grace, so that he could say, "This is what God has done for me, and He can do the same for you."

We forget that the minister is human and limited. He will make mistakes. Don't expect your pastor to be perfect or excel in every area of the ministry. Don't be shocked when you discover that your pastor is not a combination of an outstanding Bible teacher, a spirited evangelist, a compassionate pastor, and an able administrator all wrapped up in one person. Pastors simply do not come that way. When we read Ephesians 4:7, 11-12 we discover that the Lord doesn't even expect that of ministers because "some are called to be prophets, some teachers, some pastors, some evangelists." You have called the person that you feel God has sent to you, and your job is to encourage your pastor to develop the gifts God has given.

Several years ago the *Christian Index*, the weekly publication of the Georgia Baptist Convention, printed an article that helps us to identify with the expectation that we sometimes have of the pastor. It reads like this.

> After hundreds of years, a model preacher has been found to suit everyone. He preaches exactly 20 minutes and then sits down. He condemns sin, but never hurts anyone's feelings.
>
> He works from 8:00 AM to 10:00 PM in every type of task from preaching to custodial service. He makes $60 a week, wears good clothes, buys good books regularly, has a nice family, drives a good car, and gives $30 a week to the church. He also stands ready to contribute to every worthwhile charity.
>
> He is 26 years old and has been preaching for 30 years. He is tall and short, thin and heavy set, and handsome. He has one brown eye and one blue eye, hair parted in the middle with the left side dark and straight and the right side brown and wavy.
>
> He has a burning desire to work with teenagers and spends all his time with older folks. He smiles all the time with a straight face because he has a sense of humor that keeps him seriously dedicated to his work.
>
> He makes 15 calls a day on church members, spends all his time evangelizing the unchurched, and is never out of his office.

Studies continue to be made concerning frustrations of pastors. Insight into why so many leave the ministry each year is constantly sought. Could it be because many churches expect their pastor to be superhuman, a composite leader that no man can ever be?

In the early church the deacons supplemented the pastor's ministry. When the pastor was weak or spread out too thin, or was unable to do, deacons were selected to pick up the slack.

You will save your church many problems if you will remember that your pastor is human and is limited. Don't expect any more of your pastor than one can humanly be.

Our text indicates that the minister is "sent from God." This means that he has divine authorization. You have called him because you believe him to be a God-called minister. It is very important that we know this because this will counterbalance the human-limited being that he is. We want to say, "If he is like me, why should I listen to him?" But you see, with divine authorization the pastor represents God, with a message from God, and we ought to treat the pastor as God's servant.

I realize the ministry has been abused and misused in recent years. We have used it to fight our racial battles. We have abused it in the political circles. We have seen it used on radio and television to build material kingdoms. We have seen it used to abuse people. But remember the Bible underlines the minister's calling and authorization in Romans 10:14-15 which reads, "But how can they call to him for help if they have not believed? And how can they believe if they have not heard the message? And how can they hear if the message is not proclaimed? And how can the message be proclaimed if the messengers are not sent out? As the scripture says, 'How wonderful is the coming of messengers who bring good news!'" It is also good that we remember that David of the Old Testament refused to kill Saul, God's appointed one. Also, you remember in I Samuel 26:7-11 these words, "The Lord forbid that I should stretch forth my hand against the Lord's anointed."

You have called your pastor, you believe your pastor to be God's servant for your church, so I encourage you to undergird your pastor. Support your pastor. "Lift up his hands," as they did the hands of Moses. Pray for your pastor.

Now if your pastor doesn't live up to God's call, if your pastor abuses authority, if your pastor allows temptation to overrule, that is a problem your pastor will have to give an account for. Let us not always be judging the pastor. Your pastor will have to give an account to God for that. And believe you me, God is neither blind nor deaf.

There is one other emphasis in this text, and it is in the seventh verse, and it indicates that the minister is "to bear witness." The pastor bears witness in all that a pastor does and wherever that ministry might dictate, in the hospital, in the pulpit, in the community, in the backyard. At the same time we must remember that our responsibility "to bear witness" is not removed with the pastor's coming. The pastor cannot do it all, and we should not expect such. The text indicates the priority is "to bear witness," and if we have called our pastor to do it, it is also our responsibility to help the pastor to do it. Now what has happened in many cases is that we have developed a lot of machinery (programs) and we expect the pastor to operate them all. Thus the pastor has such pressing demands that something is neglected and most of the time it is study and preparation for preaching and teaching and witnessing. And it appears that this is what has happened to us today. Any time the studying and preaching and teaching of God's word is neglected, the world slumps into moral decay and apathy.

As your new pastor comes soon, it is also important to remember that your pastor has come "to bear witness" to you. Therefore, I would encourage you to insist that your pastor not be a "peddler of preaching." By this I mean to insist that he preach to your human needs.

I remember in the town where I grew up a man who made pills and tonic from roots and herbs and sold his wares on the street corner on Saturday when people would come to town to shop. He was called a peddler of medicine. He claimed to have a cure for all aches and pains. But you see he had not studied medicine. He had no authorization to practice. Some laughed at him. Others were fooled by his sales pitch.

Insist that your pastor not be a peddler of preaching because some preachers do preach beautiful sermons that have no application to life. Some even preach to people who are not present. Tell your pastor that you would like to hear a sermon on forgiveness or love or assurance. Tell your pastor where you hurt, tell your pastor you are lonely or depressed or grieving. Help your pastor to know your needs.

I would also encourage you to insist that your pastor pray for you. Not to you or over you but for you. Tell your pastor what your prayer needs are. Ask your pastor to join you in praying for your needs.

It is also important that you believe in your pastor. Trust your pastor. Don't wait and express your feelings ten years later when your pastor leaves. Do it soon. Confirm your pastor. Let your pastor know that you are behind him. One of the strong evidences of your support for your pastor is revealed when you bring others to hear him preach.

Communicate with your pastor. Speak to him, call him on the telephone, write him a note. Be his friend. He needs friends; he is leaving established friendships to come to serve here. Be his friend. Help your pastor to make friends.

Pray for your pastor. Make it part of your prayers to pray for your pastor. Maybe that prayer could be similar to this one:

Father, our pastor will need your help today,
He will walk the halls of our hospitals,
He will watch a mother weep over her child,
He will stand by a grave side and give comfort,
He will rejoice with the parents of a new baby,
He will take a stand for what is right
    in the sight of God for our community,
He will counsel with a broken home,
He will fight with temptations,
He will be threatened with compromise,
He will be judged falsely,
More will be expected of him than he can give,
Father, today walk with our pastor.

Your church is no stronger than the working relationship of you and your pastor. To understand the pastor's calling and the task of the pastor is very important. The working together of the two is essential. The pastor cannot do it alone. Your help must be the foundation on which he builds. One of the greatest joys you will find as a Christian is to join hands and hearts with your pastor to bear witness of our living Lord.